All *of* Me

Eric L. Finnie and Ashante S. Finnie

DORRANCE PUBLISHING CO
EST. 1920
PITTSBURGH, PENNSYLVANIA 15238

Dorrance Publishing Co
585 Alpha Drive
Pittsburgh, PA 15238
Visit our website at *www.dorrancebookstore.com*

ISBN: 979-8-8860-4133-0
eISBN: 979-8-8860-4798-1

All *of* Me

*Dedicated to my family, friends, and any other supporters
who have never stop believing in me.*

*A special dedication to my kids
Eric, Ashante, and Danerica,
and my angel (grandmother)
watching over me,
Loretta Pace.*

Table of Contents

CHAPTER 1

My Heart

The Heart Never Lies

My heart explains to me that it's not possible for me to be away from
the love that you give to me that fills me with joy each day.
A feeling that is tangible and can't be broken; a love so deep its
meaning can't be spoken.
You complete me and make me whole; give me meaning, and capture
my soul.
A special love that has vitality and vivacity, something very intimate; so
intimate that when I long for it, it longs back for me.
It's a treasure that only our spirits together can uncover; a love I have
to hold, cherish, respect, and smother.
It brings tears to my eyes and butterflies to my stomach. It's so good
that sometimes I wanna say I don't want it and run from it.
I crave it; need it; want it; live for it. I'm a slave to it; feign for it;
hooked on it. I adore it.
It's voluptuous, sensual, exotic, and erotic. It makes me forget
everything else, and it becomes every topic.
This love of yours rushes me hard and stands me straight up. It burns
with a passion, and I shiver at its touch.
It soothes me; it thrills me; it chills me. It shakes me; it makes me; it
breaks me; it fills me.
Your love to me does all this and more. But it doesn't compare to what
I have in store.

First Impressions

It wasn't the way your eyes said you needed to be loved,
Or the way your voice seduced my name.
It was not the way your hair caressed your shoulders;
Not even the way you licked your lips with passion.
It couldn't have been that sexy dress that fit your every curve.
I'm almost certain it wasn't the softness of your skin against mine,
Or how you brushed the hair out of your face with your finger.
It was just the sweetness of your tone when you told me you were
tired of being alone, mistreated, and used.
It was also the smile on your face that said you wanted to trust again.
It was the long conversation we had about what things we like and like
to do.
Baby, no material thing or physical feature could ever win my heart.
It was just your personality; the very first impression of you that I got
stuck with me and blew me away.
And it's that impression that I see every time I see you, touch you, and
even think of you.
It's that impression that has made me fall in love with your spirit.
The same impression that has made me value your mind, respect your
principles, and honor your soul.
So forgive me if I ever or often mention that night we first talked,
Because it was that night that I got my first impression of you and
decided you were sent to be with me.

I Love You

I love the person you are; so different, so unique.
I love the woman you are; so lovable, so sweet.
I love the mother you are; so protective, so caring.
I love the friend you are; so giving, so sharing.
I love the worker you are; so dedicated, so determined.
I love the student you are; so cooperative, so learning.
I love the truth you are; so honest, so open.
I love the spirit you are; so enlightened, so outspoken.
I love the looker you are; so beautiful, so classy.
I love the freak you are; so seductive, so nasty.
I love the kid you are; so playful, so fun.
I love you for being you, so don't change for none.

Simply You

The way you walk, the way you talk, the way you wear your hair,
Your pretty eyes, your gorgeous smile, the way you show you care,
That delicious smell, your skin like caramel, the sexy way you think,
Your exotic curves, hypnotic lures, the way you eat and drink,
Those sweetest kisses from lips so vicious, the way you say my name,
Your softest touch, your strongest clutch, the way you keep me sane…
Now I could go on for days and days about what it is you do, to make
me feel the way I feel, or I could just say it's simply you.

I Just Want to Chill

I don't want to discuss past relationships;
I don't want to talk about ex-lovers bullshit.
Don't want to converse about what feels bad, and we won't chit chat
about what makes us sad.
Don't want to speak on what brings us down, and we won't ask who's
messing around.
We won't gripe about the things we hate;
We won't carry on about how much money we make.
We'll just discuss future plans together,
Then talk about making our love better.
We'll converse about what makes us smile,
Then chit chat about what drives us wild.
We'll speak of fun places we go,
Then ask should we go once more.
We'll only gripe about what's left to do,
Then carry on about how much I please you.
So it doesn't matter how much time we have to kill, or how slow it
goes by—I just want to chill!

One Love

Two hearts beating to a surrender; that is simple and sweet.
Two minds connecting on a level that is complete.
Three words taking the heart on a pleasure cruise.
Three words bringing much joy, replacing my/your blues.
Four eyes seeing a future so clear, so bright.
Four hands clutching and holding on so tight.
Five fingers caressing from head to toe.
Six senses very active, making emotions grow.
Seven days of each week to spend in each other's space.
Eight letters written taking only a second to put a smile on their face.
Nine months of eagerness bringing a bundle of joy.
Ten numbers to dial to hear the sound of their voice.
Now all this is what happiness and fulfillment is made of. Add all this together, and it equals one love.

Love

It goes way deeper and far beyond what the eye can see;
It's something internal and deep inside of thee.
Its unseen but felt with force.
It speaks a language but doesn't have a voice.
It can hurt like hell and leave a scar.
It can flood with passion and control your heart.
It can take your mind to marvelous heights.
It can take your emotions on the wildest flights.
It has no smell; you can't see or hear it come.
It can be as light as a feather or weigh more than a ton.
It has no color but can shine so bright.
It can be as light as day and as dark as night.
This wonderful thing that I speak so highly of
Is the most precious gift I can give you: love!

The Eyes Say It All

It's something about the way you look at me, the technique in your glare;
Just that certain twinkle in your eyes whenever you stare.
There's a calmness in your glance that tells me you're at peace
With this thing that we share, and what we could be.
Even when they're closed, they still have that special gift;
To give me certainty and give my heart a delightful lift.
So look at me, my tender pet; let your eyes seduce me hard,
Because from the first moment our eyes met, you had me from the start.

My Better Half

I'm not looking for a woman of the moment, a fantasy friend, or a
night of intimate lust. What I want is also what I need: a woman to
love and trust.
A princess full of joy, happiness; one in need of a prince. A goddess
with priorities, goals, and plenty common sense.
An angel willing to build a paradise and love me to no end. A
tenderoni to be my sidekick, my lover, my very best friend.
Someone into sports, movies, music, who just loves to chill, just us
alone. A precious gem who doesn't mind making me a happy home.
One of character and a sense of humor is a must—a lady in every
sense of the word; and a love for kids is a plus.
A woman who is not afraid to be exotic for her man, wearing lingerie,
even getting into role play, or making love in chocolate, whipped
cream, or on the beach in the sand.
So if you feel that these requirements are not too much for a man to ask,
then do me a favor and become a life saver and become my better half.

The Proposal

Hold my hands, look into my eyes;
Find a place within my warmth, let me ease your mind.
Make yourself a home in my heart, let me care for you;
Never walk alone again, let me be there for you.
There will be no more lonely days; no more hopeless dreams. No
more lonely years—now you and I are a team.
Take my joy, make it your for life;
Caress my soul, let me be your high.
Bathe in my passions, make my dreams a reality;
Kill all your worries, leave your doubts/casualties.
We'll create a new love made of truth and devotion,
Then share a new life of fulfilment and explore every emotion.
Stress no more, for I vow to carry thee,
And give a lifetime of happiness if you'll marry me.

The Vows

Standing here looking in your eyes only makes me more and more sure
of how willing I am to take on our future together and build a love
that will endure.
All that comes forth—good times and bad; because the moment you
first looked in my eyes, I knew what I had.
I'll be all that you need and there when you need it. I promise to love
you unconditionally, and value your love and never mistreat it.
So as we take this path and start a new life, this will forever be the
most important day to me: the day you decided to be my wife.

First Dance

Come here, baby. I need you in my space.

Now that you're my wife, there's no other place.

Besides, they're playing our song,

So I could hold you in my arms and move all night long.

Your softness is weakening, and your smell gives me chills.

Your beauty becomes you; it inspires me, and I love the way it feels.

Slowly, baby girl; we've got nothing but time.

And as we glide across the floor, time becomes blind.

Everyone is watching as we remain in our trance,

Savoring every second of our first but not last dance.

The Honeymoon

Finally I've got you alone and to myself. A week on an
Island; not a thought of anyone else.

Yes! And you're looking delicious—good enough to eat.
And I can't wait to lick you from your head to your feet.

Lie here in my arms as we listen to our favorite tunes,
Then we'll dance slow outside under the glow of the moon.

Then go for a moonlit swim in waters clear as day. I'd
Read you my poetry and take your breath away.
Every morning will be golden, and the remaining
Of each day will be priceless,
Because we'll feed each other
Breakfast in bed, and in the evening, we'll get lost in each
Other's charm, passion, and niceness.

On our last day and night, we'll visit all the sights
And collect souvenirs to mark the start of our new life.

Then it's off to the real world, where things will get harder
Soon. But we'll never forget our beautiful honeymoon.

True Treasures

You cannot replace the beautiful people that God has put in your life.
Once they're gone, there is no replacement, so before you lose them,
think twice.
It's very hard to find someone whose not judgmental or someone who
will be true till the end,
Or someone who will care, love you, and be a real friend;
A person or people who will tell you when you're wrong as well as
when your right,
Someone who'll be there during your most calm days as well as your
stormiest nights.
A human being who defines the word loyalty,
Someone who's going to be there along for the trip, no matter how
frustrating or long the voyage may be.
These people are gifts, heavensent like
Guardian angels, and can affect your life in large measures.
They mean more than any material thing, for they are true treasures.

Just a Portion

I don't need a lot, just enough to get me by.
I only want a little buzz, not so much that I'll be high.
Just give me a taste; a sample would do me just fine.
I only want to see what it's like—it doesn't have to be mine.
Just let me have a handful; a smidge; a squirt,
So I'll know how it feels and just to know how it works.
Just explain to me what it does; educate me on its motives.
Help me understand why it's so wanted and so explosive.
Just make me wise, and I'll proceed with caution.
I want love in the future, but for now, I just want a portion.

No Such Thing as Distance

When the heart speaks and demands
To be heard, and feelings are obvious without
Saying a word;
When a song reminds you of
What you share, and the thought of that person
Makes you stare;
When you laugh to yourself at
A private joke, and you stare at a picture while you read the letter
He or she wrote;
When you touch yourself and
Feel them inside, and you buy something sexy to wear that you think
He or she might like;
When with 10 little numbers, you can hear
That person's voice, and you receive a package in the mail that makes
Your eyes moist;
When a CD of your favorite slow songs puts
You in the mood; when you cook that person's favorite food;
No matter what situation may
Cause you despair.
I'm with you no matter how,
When, or where.
What I'm saying is that if I seem
To be persistent,
It's because I believe that when it comes to love, there is
No such thing as distance.

I Have the Biggest One

I have the biggest one, and I know how to
Control it. You can grab it if you want to,
But be extra careful when you hold it.

It's a very essential part of my body, and
It performs it's many different tasks well.
But when rejected, it gets soft and hurts like hell.

But still I have the biggest one; there's no
Other like it. And when it speaks, I just
Listen and never try to fight it.

So remember when you're conversing
About all the special people you've met
And you mention their hearts, say I have the biggest one yet.

A Long Letter

Dear Sweetness,

When you feel sick, I feel sick. When you feel pain, I feel pain. The oneness I feel with you calms me and makes me feel whole. Love me, princess, allow all that I am feeling to consume you, just as it has driven me . Let your love travel through my most passionate mysteries. Allow our hearts to join and become our playground, form an unbreakable unity that will last an eternity.

Your lovemaking sets me on fire. Let me scorch your deepest insides, then have my wonderful essence soothe your burns. Hold me, baby! I'll kiss your mountains and lick your caves. Whisper your desires in my ear, scream your passions. Love me in every way, precious, and I'll return that love over and over again.

Yours Forever,
Eric

Something About You

My life is a much more peaceful and sweeter place with you in it, no
matter how much we argue, fuss, or fight. Because I know we'll make up
within a minute and turn a hopeless moment into a beautiful future life.
Each second we spend in each other's space leaves no room for
mistakes and flaws. I see part of me when I look in your face,
and I want to pamper, love, and please you with no special cause.
If I couldn't touch you, I'd touch the thought of you, and let your
graceful charm caress my ailing mind. I'd thank God and heaven above
for every part of you, and never forget the day He made you mine.
You have a serenity that is intoxicating and essential, so full of
endurance and alacrity, it makes me weak. And to this serenity,
I surrender and give myself complete.

Straight Up

I'm not here to feed you bullshit, or tell you what I think you want to
hear. My only agenda is to please you, baby, and always be sincere.
I actually care about all that involves you, and I look forward to seeing
what, what we share can evolve to.
So please don't misunderstand; my intentions are and always will be
good. And if it's not too much trouble, allow me to prove that I could
Be what you need in a man to make you feel secure. But I don't want
to rush you, so tell me if you are not sure,
Because, see, I'm willing to wait for what I believe is meant to be,
especially when I feel so much that you were meant for me.
So the only way I know to come is honestly, real, and never try to fake
love, because the only way to have something true is to always be
straight up!

I'll Remember

I need to thank you for being you and for being there when I needed
someone to care; I'll never forget how thoughtful you were and how
much of yourself you were willing to share.
When needed, you were tough and stood your ground on certain
issues; but you were willing to listen and sometimes understand when
I didn't agree with you.
You are truly a humble person and as classy as they come. Your
personality is so breathtaking, you're compared to none.
I need you to know how you helped and put my mind at ease. Little did I
know that God would send me an angel when I got down on my knees.
So read every word of this and take it to the heart, because if we have
to ever go our separate ways, I'll always remember how you helped me
when my world was falling apart.

True Beauty

I just want you to know that I watched you while you were sleeping. I ran my fingers through your hair as I realized that I would not be whole without you. In your peaceful state, I noticed your infectious smile. I put my arm around you, and I could feel your heart beat against my arm.

As I reminisced about all the good times we shared, you shifted, and for a brief moment, you looked back at me and smiled. Realizing that I was there, you moved closer, and I felt loved, wanted, and needed. I must admit, I did not know until that very moment what I had in my life. I am thankful! You mean the world to me! And I'm glad I took this time to actually pay attention to you, precious, because it was right then that I saw your true beauty.

I love you!

Amazing

Every now and again, you meet someone who leaves you in awe—
someone strong willed and gifted; someone whom within has the
ability to withstand all and still stand tall.
A person who has struggled to maintain and just brushed it off as if
it's nothing to me; someone who has been abused and knows
everything that suffering can be.
A unique being who accepted the bad with the good, someone whose
conversation could put you in a positive mood.
This person will give up their last to help another and do without for
that moment, sacrificing self for others.
A wonderful spirit that has been built back up from being battered and
broken down; a big heart that was caged in but is open now.
This person judges no one but accepts criticism as a gift, taking on
responsibility to them is a special uplift.
This person is simply amazing!

Someone You Can Relate To

When you reach a certain age, time is of the essence.
You want someone whose sure of themselves in your life and in your presence—
Someone who doesn't regret where they've been, respects where they are, and has their mind set where they're going;
A person who's about learning and understanding you as the relationship and love keeps growing.
Someone who wouldn't die for you but would convince you that both of you have something to live for;
That special person who hardly ever receives anything but is always giving more.
A person who'll give their heart freely and is not afraid to
Share their love with a person whom they can relate to.

All I Have

I am not a doctor; I don't have a medical degree.

I'm not a lawyer; I can't defend any case successfully.

I am not a pilot; I can't fly you all around the world.

I am not a psychic; I can't tell you how the future unfurls.

I don't have a fancy car or big house for us to share.

I don't make promises I know I can't keep; I'll never say I will when I can't be there.

What I have is a kind heart, and I offer this to you;

And it comes with plenty of love, unconditional, through and through.

Just Doesn't Make Sense

It would be silly for me to assume you're easy just because of the type of clothes you wear, and it would be crazy to say you're materialistic because your hair and nails are in such good care.

It would be ridiculous to think you're only out for money cause you want a man who can provide; or it would be even more idiotic for me to act like I can when I know I can't give you what you need to survive.

It would be outrageous to believe you couldn't love because your past relationships didn't work, just as it would be stupid of me to not want to try just because I've been hurt.

It would be premature to make promises that I don't know for sure I can keep, and it would be immature not to think of you and your feelings before I speak.

It would be so absurd for me not to want to be with you because of some stories I've heard, and it would be preposterous for me to use that against you before you can say a word.

It would not be me to do any of these things without thoroughly being convinced, so to not want you in my life just doesn't make sense.

Try Again

Although we're not being honest with each other, I have to be honest
with myself. I know it's hard to say goodbye, but it seems that your
heart and mind are somewhere else.
But let's not end this on a bad note, because your friendship means so
much to me, and somewhere along the line, we lost sight on what a
friendship is supposed to be.
That's why before we go further, we must take a step back and try and
find what we've lost, so we can figure out where we're at.
Please understand that my love for you has always been legit, and it's
that love that won't let me just quit or forget,
Because I still believe that deep inside, we belong together, but I'd
rather we be with someone else if that is what makes us feel better.
So this is really not a break up; we're just starting over as friends. You
know—new beginnings, new experiences, and hope for a better end,
so one day we can try again.

I Am Content

If was lost, my mind was clouded, my heart was in pain, my eyes showed a mystery that I thought would remain unsolved. Loneliness was used as the conversation piece whenever someone spoke of me; I searched, begged, and pleaded for God to send me someone to share my world with. I tried clubs, supermarkets, laundry mats, churches, chat lines, and hookups through friends.

Sure enough, I'd been in love several times, but these were harsh lessons about love, honesty, trust, commitment, and sacrifice. It taught me that there are no guarantees when happiness is involved. Mistakes; I've made plenty. Perfect; I've never been. My judgement hasn't always been accurate, my intentions weren't always good, and my priorities were almost never in place. I was lost.

Then you appeared in the blink of an eye—I was captured by your essence; mesmerized by your heavenly glow. I was drawn in when you spoke. Your grace and class were unmatchable. Not even comparable. Your eyes said to me, "I'm yours!" My heart said to you, "Yes, you are!" Your lips didn't even move, when I heard: "I'll love you forever." From that moment on, you've given me joy, happiness, wonderful moments, hope, and all of the love I had been craving. And now I am content.

Questions Within Our Hearts

How can we expect this to work when, after all, we've never even met?
How can someone you've never had a chance to touch or hold be so
very hard to forget?
Why do we live so far apart when we both know we belong together?
Why is it that when I'm down, only the sound of your voice can make
me feel better?
Who will be the first to move and show how much they love the
other? Who will make the sacrifice, so we can be with one another?
When will things change and become right for the both of us? When
will we be able to share what we have, so our hearts can notice love?
What else is there left to say to each other when there is so much to be
done? What will become of our love if we never get to share it with
that special someone?

The Little Things

I love how you always check to see if I need anything or if everything's okay, and the way you touch my face before you walk away.

I've always admired how you've made sure I was prepared for work, and how you want to pamper and take care of me if there is a part of me that hurts.

You make me crazy when you put on something I like to see you wear. You turn me on when you run your fingers through your hair.

The way you keep the house clean and prepare my favorite meals, even if you know I can do it myself; how you remind me there are things to do when my mind is somewhere else;

How you're always relaxed when my homies come around and go out of your way to make sure they're all comfortable; and you never clown—

All these things are simple, but these are the things that count. The little things I remember the most, because they add up to large amounts.

Love Is

That whisper in the ear that makes a person smile,
That tear of joy that slides down the face on only happy occasions,
The call at any time of the morning just because a person is thinking
of another,
Flowers and chocolates sent to the job just for being you,
Rose pedals spread throughout the house,
Celebrating the first time you did everything with a person,
Being the first person on site when a person is feeling down or sick,
Sacrificing your happiness to make another happy,
Sitting and talking about nothing in general,
Being able to know when something is wrong,
Opening doors, pulling out chairs, lightening cigarettes,
Complimenting that person often,
Being spontaneous on any given day,
Planning a special day just for the two of you,
Getting through the hard times together,
Understanding and respecting when that person needs space…
That's what love is to me!

Letting Go

I'd end this relationship in a heartbeat if I saw that it was making you unhappy, because I wouldn't be happy if you were sad or constantly mad at me.

I understand that love comes with uncertainness and pain. But if things that bother us can't be worked out, then the love will never grow or gain.

Plus your friendship has always been and will always be the most important thing to me, and my heart can't take watching you suffer through what my eyes can plainly see.

I would gladly wish you well and hope you find what it is you need, then I would pray that whatever that is brings you joy and sets your heart free.

Therefore, I will not hold you back or keep you in an uncomfortable place. Losing you will hurt, but helping you find happiness fills me with faith.

I truly believe that if I try to keep you in something you're not feeling, you'll never know. That would destroy me or hurt me much more worse than letting go!

CHAPTER 2

My Mind

Free Your Mind

It takes time to change the essence of man, and anything worth having is worth waiting for. Each passing day is a test, and your next moment is worth praying for.

Wishes, dreams, goals, and ambitions make life worth living; experiences are what get us through. Situations and obstacles are inevitable, but choices are left up to you.

Happiness and joy are rewards for the spirit; a piece of mind is an accomplishment. To have love is to have lived; to find peace is to find comfort within.

So take life one day at a time and make each moment count. Let your stress lay to rest, and be blessed in large amounts.

Unconscious Mind

An unconscious mind is a dangerous thing; it can produce the most
threatening entity.
It could be very explosive and ruin a person potentially.
It's a dark place: unmerciful, unbalanced, and unrevealing.
It's a clouded space; so confused, so misused, and so unforgiving,
It can bring out the worst in the best people, and for the bad people,
there's resistance.
It will show you a side of yourself that you never knew existed;
It can make the strongest man weak, and the weakest man a
Monster.
When conscious again, it's too late—you're buried beneath something
you can't get from under.
There's no progress with it, no ideas, no goals.
There's no pride, no dignity, no respect, no soul.
Not a thought, not a memory, not a feeling, just empty;
Just angry, just pain and self-pity.
So be aware of who you cross, because it's possible that, within time,
you could end up face to face with a person containing a dangerous
Unconscious mind.

A Moment of Clarity

We all need downtime, time to unload and unwind; to search for a
certain something that we rarely have time to find.
In the state of confusion, stress can take hold, so you get caught up in
the moment, and you feel it in your soul.
You have so many questions but never any answers, and it lingers
inside you and eats you up like a cancer;
Causes headaches and migraines; high blood pressure and chest pains;
just worries and concerns that no one can explain,
And to get your mind right, you need some you time just to evaluate
and meditate. Analyze all the problems, prioritize, and get'em straight.
It's what I call a moment of realness; a moment of self-therapy.
A moment of exploration, moment of soul-searching; a moment
of clarity.

Information

Each one, teach one; help somebody grow.

Inform them; please, let somebody know.

Give them a little wisdom; educate their mind.

Lay some knowledge down; don't keep it all confined.

Paint them a picture; let your voice be the paint. Make it vivid in
description; carve it in their brain.

Blow them out the water with what you've
Experienced and learned.

Talk to them and make them understand that it's their turn.

Open someone's eyes; let them see the light.

Coach them on how not to use their fist but use their mind to fight.

Point them in the right direction; don't let them go astray.

Aggravate them until they get it—don't let them walk away,

Because once they have it, they'll understand why you had to insist

That they take in all the information and how powerful it is.

The Good Die Young

The good die young, not even having a chance to grow yet; not able to see the world, not old enough to know it.

Still innocent and sweet, lovable and adorable; curious and full of life, full of joy and explorable.

So fragile and honest, exciting and courageous; free spirited, uplifting, infectious and contagious.

All of this taken away by the carelessness of another, bringing pain beyond compare to a father and mother.

Somebody's seed, somebody's daughter, somebody's son; A piece of somebody's family tree chopped off and gone.

The bad prevails, and evil lives on. Hope is destroyed forever when the good die young.

Do You (Be Yourself)

You can't please everyone! And those you do are usually the ones who disappoint you.
Friends are never what they seem to be when you need them to come through.
Peer pressure exists for those of all ages, plus the world is a competitive place;
The need to fit in or belong leaves priorities misplaced.
Your dreams are sometimes shot down by those who are afraid to dream.
Deceit is a quality possessed by many, so be aware of plots and schemes.
Once again, you can always be true to yourself and always do you.

Life's Fucked Up Like That

I'm not a politician; I don't follow the government. I just observe,
listen, and learn, and notice the suffering.
High officials seem to get off on being cruel and unfair. And I'd be a
fool to lose my cool, expecting them to care.
The world is changing little by little; there's nothing I can do,
Except adapt, sit back, and watch it unfold like you.
Back in the days, the cost of loving was low, but times were hard as hell.
Nowadays, it's a struggle to live, and you can't afford what's for sale.
They say put God first, have faith in Him, and pray for what you want,
But the next man has the devil in him and is ready to pull a stunt.
Unfortunately some things never change, and lost time can never get back.
That's just the way things work; life's fucked up like that.

This Is My World

This is my world,
My world to conquer,
And there are no obstacles big or strong enough to stop me.
All negative energy, I have turned into positive thinking;
To determination, goals, and visions of success.
My destination is always in view because I am focused.
My dreams, ambitions, self-satisfaction, and knowledge are my
motivation.
I am unstoppable.
There is nothing I am not willing to learn;
There are no limits I am not willing to cross;
There are no heights I am not willing to climb.
I have passion;
I have will;
I have drive.
My brain has become the sponge of information,
Soaking up everything I need to know to prepare me for the world,
To prepare me for challenges,
To prepare me for the unexpected,
To prepare me for the world.
This is my world!
The world is mine!

Crack

I mess up people's minds. Yes! I get in their heads. I make them feel so alive, then leave them for dead.

With me, you lose weight cause you refuse to eat. With me, you'll miss nothing, because you'll refuse to sleep.

I'll take your self-esteem; your self-respect will follow. If you chill with me today, you'll be a slave to me tomorrow.

Then I'll introduce you diseases, scandals, and breaking the law. Then I make you lose your job, home, and all you were

Living for.

Some prefer my twin sister; they say she's a little lighter and cuts them some slack. But we're both here to destroy you:

She is Cocaine, and I am Crack.

I'm Crying Out

I'm not insane! I'm not violent, stupid, illiterate, confused, or lost. I'm in a state of mind where I can't help myself, and a bottle or can is my only way out.

So when I get drunk to the point where emotions start to low, don't fear me; reach out to me. If you care, let me know.

Hold me and tell me I'll be alright; just talk to me and let me know I'm not alone in life.

Cause I can handle my liquor; I can't handle cancellation and rejection. All the constant throwing up, headaches, blackouts, and losing direction. It's a pain in the butt, but that doesn't compare to the pain of feeling unwanted or unappreciated, or thinking no one cares. So I look at the bottle as my closest friend who will always comfort me and always has the answers to my most difficult questions and will never run from me.

But in reality, I'd stop drinking cold turkey, on the spot, if someone would notice my pain and give me some help to keep me from crying out again.

Betrayal

How can I be so naïve and be attracted to what I so much despise, something that I have not just heard about, but I am seeing with my own eyes?
It could be the fear of being alone and having no one, or it could be that I've opened myself up to be misled by emotion. Maybe I feel alive like I've been born again, or just maybe thinking I'm needed is really worth something.
I've threatened to leave so many different times, but I'm still here, putting up with deceit and lies.
Can't help but blame myself; it seems I have failed and become a victim of a treacherous thing: betrayal!

Reasons

I did it because I was weak and didn't have the strength to refuse. I did
it because it made me see things from a different point of view.
I did it because I was alone, without a soul to tell me it's wrong. I did it
because it made me a king and gave me my thrown.
I did it because the person I am is not the person I want to be. I did it
to step outside myself and take a look at me.
I did it to impress others, to be accepted and loved. I did it because,
for me, it creates a whole new world.
I did it for money; I had no respect. I did it because it helped me when
I was stressed out and depressed.
I did it because I had failed at everything else. I did it because I had
disrespect and disregard for myself.

Freedom

In my dreams, I see reality; a truth beyond this world.

In my spirit, I find rest; no stress to work my nerves.

In my heart, I know love—the unconditional kind.

In my bones, I feel weary; I need to unwind.

In my eyes are visions of success, and I proceed to make it real.

In my soul is the motivation; the passion behind what I feel.

What I'm saying is, in my world, being behind these walls don't bother me none,

Because in my mind, all I see is freedom.

Life Is What You Make It

First, I, Eric Lamar Finnie, have not been appointed by God as judge
of anyone. But I do see what I see and hear what hear; this is my opinion.
Brothers and sisters seem to be waiting for what they think is owed to
them, people who've stopped along the way and refuse to go again
The truth of the matter is, we are owed nothing. We are privileged
to be here, and we all are here for a purpose. We must make this
purpose clear.
Sure, we can make our own decisions, but our destiny is not in our
control. Life is a test you either pass or fail and let it unfold.
Unfortunately, on Judgement Day, there will be no do-overs or second
chances, so you learn. Use what you've learned, adapting to life's ups
and downs and advancing.
So who are we to blame society or the other man for holding us back?
Or the Mexican for taking our jobs we are often late, for but he is so
willing to be at?
For sure, every inmate in prison is innocent, and maybe having a
liquor store on every corner plays a part. But it's your choice to
commit a crime or buy that bottle, and that choice is never too hard.
Crack, AIDS, teenage moms, murderous kids, and unemployed
individuals are all choices to be made. In life, if you choose any of
these, your life is sure to fade.

Focus

Staying focused is a hard thing to do, because there are so many people who find pleasure in confusing you.

But when you know what you want and follow your own path, stay motivated, determined, and never look back…

Your blessings will come; just never give up faith. Learn and know people, but always be safe.

Be real at all times, and at all times, stay true. Remember, respect is good for all, or no respect is due.

Karma is important; what you put out, you get back in. What you believe in, stand firm on and never bend.

Keep your eyes on those close to you; family, friends, and associates, cause these are usually the ones who help you forget what the focus is.

Wisdom

Anger, rage, and hostility are defeated by discipline. Honor, respect,
and patience are virtues of gifted men.
Give more than you receive, and your blessing will come. Cherish any
and everything you have, because it's the world compared to those
who have none.
Ask questions before you accuse; be understanding before you judge.
Be honest with yourself, and others opinions won't matter much.

Mighty Dollars

Money rules the world, but it's the root of all evil. It induces greed, encourages envy, feeds power, assists hate, and misleads you.

It is the legal drug that mostly everyone in the world craves. It makes the weak out of fools and the strong out of slaves. It comes into your life, and just when you get relax with it, it becomes stressful, because just enough causes misery and too much causes loneliness and increases unhappiness.

A dollar won't get you spit; a million won't even last long. And people get killed quick, trying to get their cash on. It keeps people laid up bitter, paranoid, and feeling sick, trying to figure out who they can trust and who they should be dealing with.

So remember there are important things that can't be bought—like love, happiness, and the power of thought. So while you're waiting to get rich so you can pop that mighty collar, don't forget to respect that mighty dollar.

Memories

They are like mental pictures that last forever: some brighten your day and make you feel better.
Others bring pain and cause you grief; many are so awful, they still cause you disbelief.
The ones I like the most are the ones that make you smile, like the ones of you spending time with your child.
To make a long story short, they all serve a specific purpose, and when everyone and everything is long gone, the memories are well worth it.

No Loyalty

I'm not here to judge anyone; I just see what I see. And my eyes are not lying when they say that no one is going to help me.

I'm out here on my own; just me, myself alone. And it's hard to do right when you've just been doing wrong for so long.

Trust—what the fuck is that? There are no friends when in need. People will camp out where you sleep; soon as you snooze, they're on the creep.

Men, love no hoes; trust no bitch; don't confide in no sluts, cause they only good for three things: that's head, a fuck, and spending your bucks.

Now family! That's a different story. They're supposed to have your back, but when you need them, you don't see them and don't know where the fuck they're at.

Loyalty! There's none of that. These fuckers are trifling and demented. Turn your back to the bastards; they'll stick the knife in and bend it

Till it breaks! So don't mistake a backstabber for a true motherfucker. Can't feel what I'm saying? Keep playing and watch what the game do to you, motherfucker.

Incarcerated Minds

I'd rather face the hard times before I sell my soul to the devil,
But these young fools today are on a whole different level.
Can't stand to see another man having shit,
Don't have enough sense to go out and get your own, so you want
what the next man gets.
Fucking brains on lockdown, scared to face reality;
Battlefield left with casualities, families left with shattered dreams.
They couldn't care less about our kids' lives; they get high then go and
murder innocent people in the midnight.
See'em in the courtroom, looking sick, knowing they failed.
No where to go on deathrow, headed to hell.
In my dreams, I see unity;
When I awake, I see horror in every damn community.
I've seen a lot of sick shit in my lifetime. I'm surprised I made it.
These fools ain't in their right mind—thinking process is incarcerated.

My Mind

You want my mind, then enter the maze and explore every mystery;
every dramatic phase.
Be dazzled by my intellect and amazed by my endurance. Let the
information guide you and provide you with assurance.
So here! Take it, but be sure not to overload, because too much of my
mind could cause your brain cells to explode.

CHAPTER 3

My Soul

A Prayer (Father, Forgive Me)

Now I lay me down to sleep, I pray the Lord my soul to keep.
If I should die before I wake, at least I can set the record straight!

I've sold weed; I've sold crack. I've snorted cocaine and guzzled
cognac.
I've beat down men and women, too; haven't killed, but shot at a few.
I've told lies and bent the truth, been involved in crime since my
youth.
I've stole things and broke in homes. I've deceived love ones for so long.
I've conned people just for fun. I've left people hanging when they
had no one.
I've slept with women three or four at a time. I've took from people
what I knew wasn't mine.
I've made promises I never planned to keep. I've thought of killing
people in their sleep.
I've spit in faces, burned down a couple of places; I've gotten away in
dangerous car chases.
I've cheated on taxes and run from car crashes. I've given false names,
ages, and addresses.

So forgive me, Father, for all that I've done. Please show me mercy.
Will you please spare me some?
Allow me to wake for days after this. I'll repent all my sins, starting
with this list.

AMEN!

God's Will

It is what I've been looking for, what I so much deserve. It has the wisdom to guide me; it is what I am willing to serve.
It is what I want to feel deep in my soul. It is what I will cherish until the day I grow old.
It is what will ease my mind and refresh my spirit. It is what will protect me; no harm will come near it.
It will be every breath I breathe and every thought I think. It will guide me to happiness; it won't let me sink.
It will help me rise above all life's adversities. All the money in the world doesn't equal what it's worth to me.
When I'm lost, it finds me and brings me back. When I'm lonely, it comforts me and helps me relax.
With it, I am brave with courage and strength. Without it, I'm a slave to misery and confinement.
It will never betray me; it will always come real. It is all I'll ever need: it is God's Will!

America's Nightmare

What turns a man into a stone cold killer, a psychopathic,
schizophrenic, cold-blood spiller?
What makes him go berserk and open fire or go for the throat with a
blade or a wire?
What turns all the good inside him into evil, making him snap and
start hating people?
What makes him feel good, just to see pain? What makes him think
that it's normal and not insane?
What makes him think it's okay to cause grief? What makes him look
at killing as a release?
What makes him do what others wouldn't dare? What turns him from
a dream child into America's nightmare?

What's a Man to Do...

When I've experienced the worst and lived to tell?
When I've been frustrated and still work hard as hell?
When my hard work brought me no appreciation?
When I'm put without a choice in a certain situation?
When my woman won't even try to understand?
When she won't butt out and let me be a man?
When I'm broke with no job and my kids need food?
When they need their learnings, and I can't afford school?
When my mom gets sick, the woman who took care of me?
When she needs me to be there, but I can't be?
When I'm going to a funeral twice a year?

Blood of My Brother

Another homie died; I can't take this shit. I'm trying to be strong, but
I'm faking it, cause I know deep inside, I'm going to miss my
brother—the laughing, drinking…damn, I wish my brother was still
alive, and I refuse to let it go. And will I survive another day now that
my friend is gone?
Should I take revenge, or should I let it be? I really can't think straight,
but I think carefully. I see his family, and they seem to be doing well. I
peep myself, and I'm trapped in this living hell. Why can't I let go and
take this as a lesson?
Maybe he's telling me, and I don't hear what he is stressing.
Nevertheless, it's hard when you've been affected so much by another.
That's why I'll forever mourn for the blood of my brother.

My Blues

I cry for all the children who have been mistreated and abused; the ones who have been beaten, murdered, and used.
I ache for all the mothers who were left alone by men who were not man enough to step up and left them on their own.
I pray for all the soldiers who were shipped off to fight against those who are prepared to die, just so we can sleep at night.
I feel for all the fathers who do their best to try and provide, work double shifts or even hustle to give their children better lives.
I hurt for all the families who lost everything in tragedies, like hurricanes, terrorist attacks, or just plain and simple casualties.

You're Nobody (Until You're Dead)

Look at me! All decked out from head to toe.
Front and center with everyone looking, I'm the star of the show.
I see people I haven't seen in a while and some I've never met,
But they've all come today to pay me respect.
My four favorite ladies are side by side:
My grandmother, mother, and two daughters with genuine tears in
their eyes.
Cousins and uncles, aunts, and friends
From both sides of the family, all packed in.
Even the people from out of town dropped in to say a word.
They sang songs of peace, the sweetest sound I ever heard.
I also see faces of some I wasn't cool with,
Distant cousins, associates, and people I went to school with.
They all came together on this glorious day;
But ain't it ironic? They came to send me away.
Before now, I couldn't find one person I could appeal to.
Now that I'm leaving, everybody wants to see me or at least act like
they're here to.

Never Had the Chance

It could all end within a second; the walls could come tumbling down.
All happiness and goodness could cease, leaving no joy to be found.
Everything could go up in flames, and love would vanish for good.
And I'd be gone leaving nothing behind; no one would know
where I stood.
What about my children? Would any of them understand why daddy
had to leave so soon?
Who'll show my daughters how to stay a lady and teach my son how
to be a man?
Will my mother miss me much after all I've put her through? Will she
remember the good in me as well as the bad, too?
I wonder if my so-called friends will show up at my funeral and say
their final goodbyes. Or will they neglect to show some respect and fill
the streets with lies?
That's why it's important that I make amends and spread my love in
advance, cause in my very last breath, I'd be worried to death if I
never had the chance.

Reality

Let's talk about reality, and what does it mean to me? When I look
around, I see that it seems to be problems that cause our society to
suffer, and at times just get rougher, and I've had enough of drug
dealers, kidnappers and child molesters. One more dies, and they've
got the best of kids of parents who didn't care none. Problems
appeared, and they couldn't bare none.
So it's one more runaway headed straight for death, and his very last
breath as he leaves is "help." The ones who survive have no one to
turn to, so they turn to crime, and this is the way they learn to survive
in the streets and live the fast life, with no self-respect, no self-esteem,
and you ask why there's another in a jail to rot or burn, with others in
the cell waiting a turn.
Maybe it leads to suicide, or a jail break; one fatal mistake when he
crosses the gate. A bullet through the air landed in his back, and he
dies on contact cause he couldn't face the facts that life is more
precious and real if you let it be dealt by the hand of reality.

Not Welcome

You're not welcome here; please, leave us alone. Let us be; we're already going through hell, struggling on our own.

We don't need your help; your assistance isn't requested. Don't want your answers, solutions; don't want to hear your suggestions.

Keep your helping hand closed; fold your open arms. Don't seduce us and confuse us with your bogus charm.

We know you exist; can't convince us otherwise. You want to treat us, then lead us with covered eyes.

But we're on to you and how you creep up on the spot. Smoking, burning up…you got the whole block hot.

Showing everything bad, but telling us it's good, trying to convince us of goals we shouldn't have, but we know we should.

Preying on the weak, trying to make non-believers out of the strong, you want us to think what you know is right when we know that it's wrong.

Just go away—leave, please. Don't stay another second. You're not wanted, not needed, and definitely not welcome!

Hell on Earth

Motherfucker, you got teachers and preachers molesting our kids.
Doctors and lawyers playing with lives for kicks.
You got murderous bombs, teenage moms; young fools not old
enough to vote carrying guns.
Fucking abortion, money laundering, extortion; kidnappings, rape,
draining spirits portion by portion.
Suicidal teens creating murderous scenes; planes crashing buildings,
out of control terrorist schemes.
Natural disasters destroying cities and lives. Wives still getting their
freak on; husbands cheating on wives.
Drug lord wars, government ploys—any man with a voice: "Let's seek
and destroy."
Courtroom shootings, city streets pollution; children learning hate
from at home schooling.
Good men going down for lazy women hang ups. Overcrowded jails;
the city don't give a plain fuck.
Hit and run accidents—some simple, some fatal. Drunk drivers,
soldiers still at war, not knowing when they'll be able
To come home. We're finding bones of people who've been dead
for years. So many fucking problems; not enough solutions, and too
many tears.
Bank robbers, store hold ups, hostages, dangerous morons on the
loose… Crack fiends, drag queens, male and female prostitutes…
So I don't worry about going to prison or being sentenced to life. My
life sentence on the outside, the devil's busy alright!

Under Siege

The world is under siege, and there is no escaping reality.

We are all victims here; our lives are filled with casualties.

You could never understand; it could never be explained. It's a war
that's gotten out of control—it could never be contained.

Police brutality; criminals are getting bolder now. Shootings in broad
daylight; murderers are getting colder now.

Terrorists strike, not fearing repercussions. Children are being
kidnapped; parents are suffering.

Molesters are set free with the urge to strike again. Survivors of
hurricanes are in search of life again.

Jobs are hard to find; the price of gas has gone to a new high. AIDS
and crack rule the streets; either way you're sure to die.

There's a gun in every hand, no discrimination of age. There's a beast
within every one, waiting to be uncaged.

Love isn't easy to find; hate is everywhere. You can smell the tension
good—sin is in the air.

Babies having babies, prisons full of fathers; mothers working twice as
hard, no time for sons and daughters.

The government is shady, unable to be trusted. The politicians are all
for self; the citizens are disgusted.

Money brings out the worst in people; for it, we lose control. Without
it, there is no survival; with it, we have no soul.

We pray to the spirit of God when we get down on our knees, but to
have faith is so hard when the devil's got us under siege.

Battered Screams and
Shattered Dreams

She was stuck in something bad; he was nothing but cruel to her, disrespectful and rude to her. And it wasn't even new to her cause she'd been through this before.

She used to keep herself together; now she looks pitiful and poor. He treated her like a whore, and she claimed he was going through some changes. All the while, her friends were telling her this fool was dangerous: she was playing herself; she'd fell off; she looked sick. She use to be thick, had brothers on her shit. But she kicked everybody to the curve cause she thought this was the one. And while she stayed home with the kids, he was in the streets having fun.

She had dreams and ambitions; goals and plans. All that went up in smoke when she chose the wrong man. Don't see him much at all; he comes and goes as he please. Now she stressing, plus she gets questions every time she leaves—accusing her; if she defends herself, then he's abusing her. He never was true to her. She use to be so fucking beautiful. But what started as a wonderful and happy scene is now an awful thing, full of battered screams and shattered dreams.

Eve of Destruction

Where was I on September 11, 2001, at 9:00 a.m.?
I was at home asleep, unaware of all the mayhem.
Little did I know, the world was about to change drastically;
At the hands of a coward and his brainwashed followers, lives would change tragically.
People died, and the lives of their friends and love ones would forever be weakened by their lost.
My TV was not on; my dreams were pleasant, and at the same time, distant U.S citizens were being murdered as I turned and tossed.
Where was I?
I was in a land where everything was great and everyone was pleasant to one another.
When I awoke, I showered, got dressed, and left with my mother.
Where was I?
With the woman who gave me life
While the mothers of the victims watched on live television as their children were being victimized.
When I finally turned the TV on, I watched in disbelief and discussion
As a beautiful day turned into the eve of destruction.

Katrina

She was a vicious vixen, determined
To destroy. Born to cause havoc, not at all coy.
Homes destroyed; lives were taken.
Families lost touch, thousands
Separated.
Some buried beneath water; others
searching for society, waiting to
Be rescued, barely keeping it
Together,
Pleading for help in order to
Survive, brought together by
Disaster becoming one in the
World's eye.
Sacrifices were made to let the
Young keep living on. Summons were
Heard—100,000 voices, one song.
It rocked my whole world, and
Changed my demeanor.
In August of 2005,
I became one with the victims of
Hurricane Katrina.

Incarceration
(The Effects on a Child)

Through the glass with tears in her eyes, in a sweet innocent voice, she asked me questions I have to answer; I have no choice.

"Daddy, are you going to come hug me? I miss you so much. Will you buy me some toys for Christmas, will you be home with us?

Is this a hospital? Why is that band on your wrist? Am I still your baby girl? Can I please have a kiss?

Why is your hair so long, and you've lost all that weight? Don't you have a comb, Daddy? Haven't you ate?

Is mommy's new friend my new daddy now? Is it me? Would you come out if my little brother was around?

Daddy, why'd you leave home… You don't love me no more? I'll be good, Daddy—please come through the door!

I'm doing good in school, got all A's and B's; made some new friends, and they're real nice to me.

I learned a new dance and heard a new song. I'll sing it to you, Daddy, if you come out, you can sing along."

Then when visiting time was up, with a tear in my eye, I said, "I'll be home soon. I love you, goodbye!"

Loneliness

Loneliness has captured me and made me a prisoner of my mind. It has taken of the now, and tomorrow is running out of time.
Please, someone notice my emptiness and guide me to fulfillment.
Lead me out of the darkness, and show me what's real again.
It is rain all the time; I never see sunshine. It's so much pain; it has never been fun time.
So tell me please, what am I to do when loneliness has claimed me and made me very blue?

Cursed

Feel what I'm feeling, and if you know where I'm coming from, lend
me some emotions cause I assure you I'm in need of some.
I feel so burnt out, like I have lived a lifetime, and as if no one else has
lived a life quite like mine.
I'm tired, worn to the core, spent, and exhausted; that pep in my step,
shine in my spirit, glim in my eyes, I've lost it.
I've been blinded for a moment; my goals are no longer in sight. And
the reason I worry so is because I feel that it's alright.

Stress

It's the reason my heart
Beats at a slow and
Steady pace. It's the
Reason there is always an
Empty look on my face.
It's the cause of all my sleepless
Nights, and it's the cause of all
My peace-less fights.
It's the reason my soul is cold and
Dark. It's the reason my world is
Lifeless and hard.
It's the reason my being here
Means so much less. It's the cause
Of my misery. It's known as stress.

Insomnia

Do you know what it feels to be restless, and very
Tired at the same time? Know what it's like to be weary
And not in their right frame of mind?
The inability to sleep, bored out of your wits, yet
exhausted to no end and uncomfortable as one can get.
Very disturbed for some reason; something isn't right.
Alert and wide awake the whole night.

My Soul

You want my soul, then get to know my spirit.
Look in my eyes and be able to know what I'm feeling before
You even hear it.

Understand where I amm and appreciate where I'm trying to go.
Don't be afraid to be yourself and say what you want me to
Know.

So here, take it and be mesmerized and uplifted, cause once you have
my soul, all control has been shifted.